POEM WITHOUT A HERO

AND SELECTED POEMS

FIELD TRANSLATION SERIES 14

Anna Akhmatova

POEM WITHOUT A HERO

AND SELECTED POEMS

Translated by Lenore Mayhew
and William McNaughton

Introduction by William McNaughton

Oberlin College Press:
FIELD Translation Series 14

Publication of this book was made possible by a grant from the Ohio Arts Council.

Library of Congress Cataloging in Publication Data
Akhmatova, Anna (translated by Lenore Mayhew and William McNaughton)
POEM WITHOUT A HERO AND SELECTED POEMS (The FIELD Translation Series; v. 14)

LC: 89–060154

ISBN: 0–932440–51–7
0–932440–50–9 (paperback)

CONTENTS

INTRODUCTION

When we began our work on Anna Akhmatova (1889–1966), having been given a tiny paperback edition of *Requiem* picked up by a friend in the Latin Quarter of Paris, very few people — outside of specialists in Russian literature — knew who she was. Happily, that situation has now changed. One could say now of this great Russian poet, as Niccolò Macchiavelli's sarcophagus proclaims in the Duomo in Florence: TANTO NOMINE, NULLAM PAR ELOGIAM — (loosely) "with a name like that, who needs a eulogy?" In 1989 Anna Akhmatova needs no introduction.[1]

We no longer have to plead a case for her as one of the greats of modern world poetry, or of all Russian poetry. Yes, in 1964 the Union of European Writers did award her the Etna-Taormina International Prize for Poetry; and yes, Oxford University in 1965 did give her a doctor's degree *honoris causa.* But since then she has, through her poetry, "convinced by her presence" — as Whitman says — and we shall limit ourselves in this introduction to the effort to get her career as a poet in focus (though our selection of her poetry must, in the main, do that); to give a sketch of her life; and to take a look at the relation of the life to the work. And she is important, we believe, not just because she is a great poet, but also because a large part of "the human experience" in the twentieth century is recorded in her poetry as nowhere else. We shall return to this point when we discuss Akhmatova as the author of "epics of persecution."

Akhmatova's literary career can be divided into three periods. Such divisions are always to some extent arbitrary, and perhaps even capricious. But we feel that something can be gained by thinking, first, of Akhmatova the lyricist and "Acmeist" poet (1912–1938); second, of Akhmatova, author of the long poems *Requiem* and *Poem Without a Hero* (1938–1949); and third, of the older Akhmatova, "wise through time and lyrical again (not narrative) with age" (1949–1966). Even the earlier collections of lyrics form, as one astute reader has remarked, "lyrical diaries," and it is impossible to disentangle the work from the life and to discuss them separately, and in the account which follows, we do not try.

The Lyricist and "Acmeist" Poet

She was born Anna Andreevna Gorenko — the cognomen "Akhmatova" was borrowed as a *nom de plume* from her Tartar grandmother — on June 11 (23), 1889, in Bolshoy Fontan, a suburb of

Odessa on the Black Sea. Her father was a naval engineer. She grew up in the St. Petersburg area, and she was to spend much of her life in the "City of Peter" and its suburbs. She came particularly to love Tsarskoe Selo, once a country palace of Catherine the Great, and in our time a small town with magnificent parks. Akhmatova's first memories are of those parks, and many of her poems were inspired by Tsarskoe Selo.

She finished her secondary education at Kiev in 1907 and enrolled as a law student at the Kiev College for Women. Without finishing the course, she moved back to St. Petersburg and attended advanced courses in history and literature at Raev, where the poet Innokenty Annensky was teaching classical literature. Akhmatova had written her first poem when she was eleven, and in 1907 she published, for the first time, a poem in the review *Sirius*. *Sirius* was edited in Paris by one of Annensky's former students, Nikolay Stepanovich Gumilev. In 1910 Akhmatova would marry Gumilev. That same year (1910), Annensky published his book of lyric poems *The Cypress Chest*, and it would have a great influence on Akhmatova's early poetry.

Such, then, were the earliest influences on Akhmatova's verse: the beautiful parks and solitudes of Tsarskoe Selo, on the one hand, and, on the other, the classical, lapidary verses of Annensky. But Gumilev was another kind of influence, and he would pull Akhmatova — and much of Russian poetry — into the twentieth century, almost ahead of the twentieth century.

Having spent her honeymoon in Paris with Gumilev, Akhmatova went back to Paris for the spring of 1911, and there she became close friends with Amedeo Modigliani. Modigliani and Akhmatova would go together to the Luxembourg Gardens, eat lunch, and trade knowledge of French poetry, quote for quote. "On rainy days," Akhmatova said, "we sat on a bench under a big black umbrella and recited from memory, in unison, Verlaine's poems. We laughed to find how many of the same poems we knew." Under Modigliani's guidance, she came to know rather well "the true Paris." In 1912 she travelled in northern Italy, visiting Genoa, Pisa, Florence, Bologna, Padua, and Venice. In 1961 she would write that her impressions of Italian architecture and painting formed during this trip were "like a dream that stays with you all your life."[2]

She and Gumilev had set up house in Tsarskoe Selo in 1911, and Gumilev proceeded to work out his literary career with diligence. In 1911 he founded the "Poets' Guild" with Sergei Gorodetsky. Out of the association with Gorodetsky came the demise of Symbolism as the pre-eminent school of Russian poetry and the rise of a new school: Acmeism. Akhmatova belonged to the Poets' Guild and to Acmeism.

The "Poets' Guild" was founded to work on the techniques of writing poetry. The word "guild" (*tsekh*) was supposed to suggest skilled medieval artisans working at their craft. Akhmatova herself describes the organization of the guild and the genesis of Acmeism:

The Guild of Poets 1911–1914

> Gumilev, Gorodetsky as syndics; Dmitri Kuz'min-Karavaev, *striaphchii* ["advocate": he was a lawyer]; Anna Akhmatova, secretary; Osip Mandelstam, Vladimir Narbut, M. Zepkevich, B. Bruni, Georgee Ivanov, Elena Kuz'min-Karavaev, Cherniavsky, M. Lozinsky. The first meeting at the Gorodetskys' on *Fontanka*; Blok was there. Frenchmen . . . ! The second time at Liza's on *Manezhnaja ploshchad'*, then at our place in Tsarskoe (Malaia, 63), Bruni's at the Academy of Arts. Acmeism was resolved at our place in Tsarskoe Selo (Malaia, 63).[3]

The scene of some of the earliest Acmeist events — including the reading of Acmeist manifestos by Gumilev and Gorodetsky — was the literary cafe "The Wandering Dog." "The Dog" figures elsewhere, too, in Akhmatova's poetry (see below, p. 121), and it has been immortalized in several scenes in Kuzmin's novel *Errants and Travellers.* "The Wandering Dog" opened late in the autumn of 1911 and was probably named after a big black dog which was always on the premises. The cafe opened at midnight three days a week. There were poetry readings, theatrical improvisations, "drink, food, flirtations — Akhmatova's poem which begins 'We are all carousers here, wantons' is certainly set in 'The Dog.' "[4]

Before we proceed with the tale of Akhmatova's life, we should probably take a brief look at the tenets of Acmeism. Acmeism has a position in the history of modern Russian poetry similar to that of Imagism in modern Anglo-American poetry, and there is a similarity between the tenets of the two schools. The Acmeists derided the "mistiness" of Symbolist poetry and proclaimed a poetry of visual vividness, of concrete imagery, of conciseness, and of words used "in the exact, logical meaning."[5] Gumilev wrote up his views as follows:

> The poem . . . has its own anatomy and physiology. First of all we see the combination of words, the meat of the poem. Their properties and qualities comprise the subject of stylistics. Then we see that these combinations of words, complementing one another, lead to a definite impression, and we note the backbone of the poem, its composition. Then we make clear to ourselves the whole nature of the images, that

> sensation which moved the poet to creation, the nervous system of the poem and in this way we come to possess the eidology. Finally (although all of this is accomplished simultaneously) our attention is taken by the sound side of the verse (rhythm, rhyme, combination of vowels and consonants) which, like blood, plays in its veins, and we comprehend the poem's phonetics . . . [6]

He had already written that Acmeism pays equal respect to all parts of the poem's anatomy. The name of the school, "Acmeism," is supposed to come from the Greek word ἀκμή, "a point, edge; the highest point of anything, the bloom, flower, prime," and the Acmeist poem has been compared to the tip of an iceberg most of which floats below the surface. Some unfriendly Russian poets claimed that the name was derived from Akhmatova's *nom de plume*, and some say that Andrei Bely and Viacheslav Ivanov one day teased Gumilev, already hostile to Symbolism, that he and his followers would, in fact, bring Symbolist poetry to the highest point (acme) of its development.[7] Akhmatova herself supports the first story and says that the group was in Gumilev's library one day looking for a name for their school, when they found in a Greek dictionary the word ἀκμή.

The Akhmatova of these days has been described to us as tall and slender, dark-haired with "deep blue eyes." She was "given to being alone"; she had been so as a child, as we can read in her poem "Willow" (see below, p. 95). She was also *ardita*, if her own description of herself as "happy sinner of Tsarskoe Selo" is true (see p. 83, below). Akhmatova published her first volume of verse in 1912: *Evening*. It was published by the Poets' Guild in an edition of 300 copies with an introduction by Mikhail Kuzmin.

Gumilev really masterminded a literary revolution that toppled Symbolism from its pre-eminence in Russian poetry. Gumilev was strong-willed, original, used to being in charge. He felt that his job was to restore *robustezza* — manliness and health — to Russian poetry: in a poem entitled "My Readers," he said

I do not offend them with neurasthenia,
I do not humble them with a soft heart
Nor do I bore them with complex symbols
about the shell of a sucked-out egg.[8]

Three of his "Acmeists" — himself, Akhmatova, and Osip Mandelstam — almost certainly occupy a permanent place in Russian poetry. Akhmatova's second book, *Rosary*, was published in 1914, and it enjoyed an enormous success.

Gumilev fought bravely in the war of 1914. He volunteered as a private and served then as officer of a cavalry unit. He fought with great distinction in the East Prussian campaign and won two Saint George crosses — as he says, speaking of himself in the third person in "Memory": "Saint George touched twice his breast untouched by bullets."

A son, Leon ("Lev"), had been born to Gumilev and Akhmatova in October, 1912. Some of Akhmatova's poems suggest, however, that between her and Gumilev there were irreconcilable temperamental differences, as there might be between two strong-willed and gifted people (see, for example, the poems on pp. 31 and 46, below). In any case they went their separate ways in 1916. In 1918 Akhmatova married the Assyriologist V. K. Shileiko. Eventually she would divorce Shileiko, too, and marry the art historian Nikolay Punin.

Akhmatova published *White Flock* in 1917 and *Plantain* in 1921. In spite of the Revolution, her reputation had never been greater. The following article, published by Korney Chukovsky in *Dom Iskusstvo* in 1921, sets her off against the famous and sensational Vladimir Mayakovsky (who for a long time was better known to American readers):

> It looks as if all Russia has divided into the Akhmatovas and the Mayakovskys. There is a gap of thousands of years between these people. And they hate one another.
>
> Akhmatova and Mayakovsky are as hostile to

> each other as the times that made them. Akhmatova is an assiduous inheritor of all the most valuable pre-revolutionary treasures of Russian literary culture. She has many ancestors: Pushkin, Boratynsky, and Annensky among them. She has that elegance of spirit and the charm that one acquires through centuries of cultural tradition. . . . Akhmatova has kept the old Russia, the motherland, "our soil." He, like a true bard of the revolution, is an internationalist, a citizen of the world, who treats with indifference the "snowy monster," the motherland. . . . He is in the street, at a mass meeting, in a crowd, he is himself a crowd. . . .
>
> I can say of myself only that . . . to my surprise, I love both of them. . . . The question Akhmatova or Mayakovsky? does not exist for me. I love both the cultural, quiet, old Russia impersonated by Akhmatova and the plebeian, violent, bravura thundering Russia of the street impersonated by Mayakovsky . . . ; they are both . . . necessary.[9]

Gumilev had been in Paris, on his way to join a Russian fighting corps on the Macedonian front at the time of the February (1917) Revolution. He went home and declared himself a supporter of the monarchy. He had already said in a poem that "I shall not die in bed between a doctor and a lawyer," and he had written:

WORKMAN

An old man stoops
Before the red-hot furnace.
He blinks red eyelids
Submissive eyelids
Over calm eyes.

The other workmen
Are home and asleep
But he is busy
He is making the bullet
That will take away my life.

When he is finished
His eyes will be gay
He will walk home under the moon
His wife is sleepy and warm
And waits for him in a big bed.

And this bullet he makes
It will whistle over the white Drina
It will search out my heart
It is my bullet.

In mortal pain, I will fall,
I will see the past as it really was,

My blood will be a fountain
Rushing to the dry, trampled grass

And the Lord will requite me
I will have full measure
For my brief and bitter life
An old man in a grey blouse
Gives it to me.[10]

Gumilev was soon arrested as a counter-revolutionary and conspirator in the "Taganstev" plot. On August 25, 1921, he was shot by a firing squad. Akhmatova may have written the poem "You will not live again" (see below, p. 65) about Gumilev's death. It was, in any case, a terrifying and tragic event for her.

In 1922 she published the book *Anno Domino MCMXXI*; in 1925 the Central Committee of the Communist Party passed a resolution forbidding the publication of her work.[11] Except for a few translations and a literary study or two, she did not publish again until 1940. She moved from Tsarskoe Selo into St. Petersburg. She lived there in an annex to the famous Sheremetev Palace on the Fontanka River, near the Anichkov Bridge. She took an interest in the architecture of Old St. Petersburg, and she occupied herself with a study of Pushkin's life and work and, of course, with her son.

Of Akhmatova's work at that point (1922), and of her position in world poetry, it would (we think) be fair to make the assessment and description of Renato Poggioli:

> Akhmatova's poems are as brief as Chinese or Japanese lyrics. . . . Each one of her collections is a lyrical diary. In this Akhmatova follows the great tradition of feminine poetry, which, from Sappho to Louise Labé, from Gaspara Stampa to Marceline Desbordes-Valmore, has always tried to tell . . . a single and simple love story . . .[12]

The Author of "Epics of Persecution"

On March 13, 1938, took place the event that was to change Akhmatova and her poetry once for all: Lev Gumilev, twenty-six years old, was arrested — probably for no better reason than, as Akhmatova's French translator surmises, that "he had the same name as his father." On that day began for Akhmatova what Carlo Riccio calls "the calvary of many Soviet mothers." The "inquisition" had already carried off some of Akhmatova's closest friends, including the poet Osip Mandelstam (a vivid account of what those days were like can be found in *Hope Against Hope*, by Nadezhda Mandelstam, Osip's wife).

Lev Gumilev was held in the old Leningrad Prison for seventeen months while he awaited sentence. And Akhmatova stood outside the prison in long lines of prisoners' relatives, almost all women, waiting to deliver packages for their imprisoned kin. Sometimes a person had to wait in line two days to get to the window through which the packages were handed in. And if one day the package was refused, it meant that the addressee had been executed. Lev was finally sentenced to exile to a desolate area on the Arctic tundra. Out of this arrest and exile of her only son, Akhmatova wrote a (for her) new kind of sustained poem: *Requiem* (see pp. 75–92, below). She had been moved by her experience to write epic poetry "not of heroism but of persecution."[13] That may be a new kind of epic in Western literature — a kind more suitable, undoubtedly, to modern times.

Akhmatova's poetry, which had been so personal and so private, suddenly became the voice of an entire people:

And I do not pray for myself only
But for all those who stood with me
In the fierce cold and in July's white heat,
Under the red unseeing wall.

In the eyes of those who waited with her under the prison, Akhmatova saw, as Carlo Riccio says, "a mother's anguish multiplied by millions." (At least until quite recently, *Requiem* had never been published in Russia, except for a brief excerpt or two.)

When the Second World War broke out, Lev asked to be released from prison to serve in the army. After some delay he was taken into the air force, and he participated in the victorious advances of the Russian troops and in the capture of Berlin. For his service he won a medal. He told his mother that, compared to his exile, life in the front lines was like a summer vacation. After the war he asked to be allowed to continue his studies of history, but he was sent into exile again, this time to the deserts of Central Asia. He was finally set free for good in 1956.

"Without *Requiem*," Riccio says, "we would not have had Akhmatova's patriotic lyrics from the war years, those lyrics that in the time of danger shouted out like an incitement to resist — an authentically *Russian* voice that no trouble and no persecution could move to repudiate the knowledge that it was an entire nation's voice, in which were the weight and the pride that it had become an historical voice." Akhmatova had been in St. Petersburg (Leningrad) at the beginning of the war and had seen the beginning of the Nazi siege there. She would fly from St. Petersburg to

Tashkent, in Uzbekistan, on September 28, 1941, and would not return until June 1944. But in St. Petersburg, as the seige began, Akhmatova began to work on the longest of her poetical works, *Poem Without a Hero* (pp. 103–149). Most of *Poem Without a Hero* was written between the end of December, 1940, and August, 1942, though Akhmatova continued to revise and work on it until 1962. In it, two times are thrown together: 1913 and 1940. Nineteen-thirteen was a time of masked balls. It was the year in which a young official, Vsevolod Knyasev (the "dragoon-Pierrot" of the poem), killed himself at the age of twenty for love of a beautiful, haughty and disdainful actress, Olga Afanasevna Glebova-Sudeikina (the 'Psyche Confusionaria' and the 'Satyress' of the poem). And as Akhmatova remembers this tragic event and other scenes and images from those days, against the Nazi seige of Leningrad, a poem develops which is "a counterpoint of digressions, a fugue of mirrors, a succession of echoes."[14]

Poem Without a Hero, though it presents to readers many of the same difficulties (and for many of the same reasons), occupies in Akhmatova's work a position similar in significance to *Four Quartets* in Eliot's work, the *Cantos* in Pound's, or *Paterson* in Williams's. Akhmatova has after all, perhaps, found for all these modernist works (as for *Ulysses*) the most descriptive title: *Poem Without a Hero.* Akhmatova refers to the poem, in the poem, as "seductive centenarian" — "centenarian" because, as she told her Italian translator, this kind of poem as a new poetic genre was born with Byron: Byron "was the first to begin his narration in the middle or at the end, with evident disregard for the connection between the various parts — Byron's poems are made up of fragments."[15] History had come into Akhmatova's voice in *Requiem*, and in *Poem Without a Hero* Akhmatova calls into the present a past that seemed never to have existed and, "breaking it up like a Cubist painting, she projects living phantoms from it onto the horror of the present hour."[16] In my opinion, the poem will present far fewer difficulties, and afford far more delight, to readers who are used to the cinema and who know McLuhan, than it did to Akhmatova's contemporaries (see, for example, pp. 106, 137). In any case no one can really "know" Akhmatova's work who doesn't know *Poem Without a Hero.* Jeanne Rude calls it "the most important of her works."

If reading *Poem Without a Hero* is like reading jottings in an intimate diary, or like participating in a scene from *Anna Karenina*, that is not, after all, so much different from the experience of reading many of her earlier short poems. It was Mandelstam who first emphasized Akhmatova's debt to the tradition of the nineteenth-century novel: "The roots of her poetry are in prose fiction . . . the concern for tangible realities, objects, and events." Akhmatova once criticized some of Solzhenitsyn's efforts at poetry by telling him, "There isn't enough *zagadka* in your poetry." *Zagadka* — puzzle or mystery. (Solzhenitsyn replied, "Yes, well, and some people think that there is too much *zagadka* in yours.") There is a fragmentary quality in Akhmatova's "jottings," in the scenes that make up her poems — especially *Poem Without a Hero.* Objects, events, and characters have been omitted. We feel their existence but can't find them on the page. The images that are there, however, have a strange aptness to this missing context — and (as the reader may have been thinking) this brings us back to Acmeism. The explanation we like best is that the Acmeist poem is supposed to be like the tip of an iceberg. Only one-tenth of its mass juts out of the water, but the submerged nine-tenths is also present. Akhmatova had often written this sort of "iceberg poem" in her pursuit of *zagadka* — telling us what she wants to tell us, shedding only such light as will render, but at the same time conceal, enchant, mystify — and the technique really comes to full flower in *Poem Without a Hero.*[17]

By 1946 Akhmatova had published a few lyrics in the review *Star.* Unfortunately, the periodical had also published some of Zoshchenko's satirical sketches of Soviet life, and Akhmatova — guilty by that most tenuous of associations — found herself in 1946 under attack from the then czar of Soviet cultural life, Andrey Zhdanov. Zhdanov attacked her in terms which were, to put it mildly, offensive: he said she was "a little bourgeoise lady who spends her time in bed or in church"; he said her poems had in them "eroticism mixed with sadness, with anguish, with mysticism"; he said her voice was "foreign to the spirit of the Soviet people." The upshot of these attacks was that she was expelled from the Union of Soviet Writers (she had had a similar experience before: see the poem "Calumny," pp. 67–68). Then her third husband, Nikolay Punin, was arrested — for his views as an art historian. He was called a "philo-Occidentalist" (he had supported avant-garde and experimental painting in post-war Russia), and he was sent to Siberia.

"Wise Through Time, and Lyrical with Age"

In this book Akhmatova's later literary production — after *Poem Without a Hero* — is represented by a number of poems. In form, Akhmatova returns to the shorter lyric poem: but these poems, like the lyrics of her early life, can be read as the story of her life, as "a lyrical diary." To us, at least, they give the life the shape of a Sophoclean drama. After the great catharsis of *Requiem* and *Poem Without a Hero*, she moves toward . . . wisdom. In the earlier of the late poems, there is a good deal of retrospection — of grief, of regret, of bitterness; of a sense of persecution. But the tone changes slowly, and Akhmatova seems to find a "peace which surpasses understanding." The "turn" may take place in the wonderful sequence about writing poetry, "Secrets of the Trade" (pp. 163–71). And that may be mimetic, for Akhmatova seems to have saved herself more than once by turning to poetry. In any case, in her later poems she can write:

> And I have carried here
>   the memory
> . . . .
> And the pure weightless flame
> Of triumph over fate.

She can find

> In me again,
>   the mystery of mysteries.

Akhmatova eventually recovered membership in the Union of Soviet Writers, and in 1964 she was President of the Union. She died at Domodedevo, near Moscow, on March 5, 1966.

We have printed the poems, insofar as possible, in their chronological order. We feel that Akhmatova's life was a great modern drama and that the best record of it is in the poems themselves. Although in a selection of poems like this one, the reader may get the impression of reading the story with some dramatic time-shifts and some major cuts, we have tried to choose the poems so that our selection, when finished, would leave readers feeling that they have heard Akhmatova's story told.

"In their chronological order" means, in general, that we have followed the ILA order. We have departed from the ILA order so that we could put Akhmatova's two longest works — *Requiem* and *Poem Without a Hero* — in sequence at approximately the point in her life at which they were written (ILA, by contrast, put *Poem Without a Hero* in their second volume). For *Poem Without a Hero*, the determining factor to us was Akhmatova's dateline at the end of the poem: "Finished at Tashkent, August 18, 1942." Such work as she did on *Poem Without a Hero* after that seems to have been entirely in the nature of revision and polishing. "The Secrets of the Trade" and "Miscellaneous

Poems" come from the so-called *Seventh Book* (cf. ILA, vol. I, pp. 249–330).

In this book we have worked on the translations, for the most part, as in our earlier collaborations.[18] In summary, WM did the philological work, and LM wrote the poems. We received from Olga Dunlop a good deal of help with problems in the Russian. We were saved from a number of errors, and our sensitivity to and appreciation of the beauties of Akhmatova's work were often enhanced, by Professor Frank R. Silbajoris of the Ohio State University, whose relentless, uncompromising, and brilliant criticism was what all translators (and, we daresay, all serious writers) always hope for and seldom find. In some cases we have, with Professor Silbajoris's kind permission, gotten this criticism into our notes, with acknowledgement.

The exception to our usual "division of labor" occurs in *Poem Without a Hero.* WM made the first version of much of it, and from this version LM worked up the translation appearing below.

We are indebted to Marjorie Hoover, Professor of German and Russian at Oberlin College, for reading our version of *Requiem* and for making suggestions and comments.

Naturally, the errors in the book are to be ascribed to us alone.

William McNaughton

from **EVENING**

He loved three things
in this life:
Vespers, white peacocks,
And old maps of America,
Didn't love children crying,
Raspberries with tea,
Or feminine hysteria
. . . And I
was his wife.

1911

My hands contract under the dark veil . . .
"Why are you so pale today?"
— Because I have sickened him
With my bleak sorrow.

How can I forget it? He went out
Staggering, his mouth twisted with grief . . .
I ran after, not touching the rail,
I found him at the gate.

And I cried out, "It was a joke,
All that: come back or I die."
His smile was calm and atrocious
And he said, "Don't stand in the draft."

1911, Kiev

from **ROSARY**

CONFUSION

I

In that burning light I suffocate —
Under those eyes like the sun's rays
I shudder: this one
Will tame me.

He leans close to tell me something . . .
And all the blood leaves my face.
May love like a tombstone
                    close over my life.

II

You don't love me?
                You don't want to look at me?
O wretch!
                How handsome you are!
And I can no longer fly,
I, who had wings
                    even as a child.
Fog covers my eyes,
Blurs faces and lights.
I see only the red tulip,
The red tulip in your buttonhole.

III

Simple courtesy requires it,
You come near, smile,
Half-tender, half-languid,
With a kiss, brush my fingers —
And from antique, mysterious faces
Eyes look at me.
And I take ten years of torment, of cries,
And my sleepless nights
And I put them in a single word —
I speak for nothing.
You go away.
                    And in my soul
Again there is emptiness
                              and light.

1913

EVENING

In the garden there were snatches of music
Wordless, melancholy.
The sharp fresh odors of the sea
Rose from oysters on cracked ice.

He said to me,
                    "I am your faithful friend,"
And touched my dress:
Unlike an embrace
The touch of that hand.

So one pets a cat or a bird
So one looks
                at well-built circus riders.
And in his tranquil eyes there was laughter
Under lashes of light gold.

And behind the drifting smoke
The voices of nostalgic violins sang
"Give thanks, thanks to the Gods —
For the first time
You are alone
                    with your love."

March, 1913

Flowers and non-living things
Make pleasant odors in the house.
By the garden beds, multi-colored vegetables
Lie in piles on the black earth.

Cold still hangs in the air
But they take away the matting from the
   seed-beds.
Near here is a pond, a pond
Whose mud is like brocade.

And the boy says to me with fear,
Very excited and hushed,
"A big carp lives in there
With his great big carp wife."

1913

Evening at my table
Is a page irremediably white:
The mimosa smells of Nice and the sun,
A large bird flies across the moon.

And I braid my hair for the night, tightly
As if tomorrow I'd still need braids:
No longer sad, I look out the window
At the sloping dunes and the sea.

What power has he then, this man,
Who doesn't even ask for tenderness!
I can't raise tired eyelids
When he calls my name.

Summer, 1913

Then for the last time we met
On the river-bank, where we always met,
And the waters of the Neva were high
And in the city, they feared a flood.

He talked of summer and how I
Am a woman-poet, and women-poets are absurd.
I remembered the tsar's palace
And the Peter and Paul Fortress.

The air was not quite ours
But like a gift of God — miraculous,
And in that hour, it came,
My last, my wildest poem.

January, 1914

TO ALEXANDER BLOK

I went to visit the poet
At noon on Sunday
It was quiet in the large room
And frosty outside the windows.

The sun was raspberry red
Over tousled blue smoke . . .
How the radiant quiet host
Looked at me!

Those eyes —
No one can forget them;
Full of caution,
I preferred not to look.

But I remember all our words
On that smoky noon, Sunday
In the high grey house
At the sea-gates of the Neva.

January, 1914

from WHITE FLOCK

My voice is feeble, my will strong
I am better without love,
The clouds are high,
                The wind blows from the mountain
And my thoughts are innocent.

My sleeplessness has gone away,
I do not sit over ashes,
The oblique hand of the clock tower
Is not a fatal arrow

And the past loses its force!
Freedom is near.
                I watch
A strip of sunlight
                Catch the wet new ivy
And I forgive . . . everything.

1912, Tsarskoe

TO V. S. SREZNEVSKAYA

Instead of wisdom — experience,
Flat brew that leaves a thirst
And youth that was a Sunday prayer . . .
Can I forget that?

So many desert roads
                    I traveled
With the one I couldn't love,
So many hours I knelt in church
For him: the one who loved me.

I become
    more forgetful than the most forgetful.
The years slide in silence
And I can never return
To unkissed lips, unsmiling eyes.

1913

How can you look at the Neva?
How can you walk the bridges? . . .
They do not find me sad for nothing,
Sad since the day we met.
The wings of the black angels are sharp,
And the last judgment is coming,
Vermilion fires like roses
Will flower in the snow.

1914

Under the frozen roof of this deserted house
I stop counting the dead days.
I read the Acts of the Apostles.
I read the Singer of the Psalms.

And the stars are blue, and the frost like feathers
And our meetings, miraculous
— each more than the last

And in my Bible
A leaf from the red maple
Marks the Song of Songs.

1915

God's angel who, one winter morning
Secretly made us one,
Still contemplates with shadowed eyes
Our untroubled life.

And for that, we love this sky,
The thin air, the new winds
And the dark branches
Against the wrought-iron fence;

For that, we love this austere
Dark city veined by water,
And our love, our separations,
Our short hours of meeting.

1914

I have learned to live a life
simple and wise
To study heaven,
and to call upon God.
And in the hours before evening
I walk in the open air
And wear away unnecessary fears.

And when burdock stirs in the gully
When red bunches and yellow
hang from the mountain ash,
I invent joyous poems
On the mortality and beauty of life.

And then I go back
and my furry cat
Licks my hand and waits,
And a live flame suddenly opens
Over the lake near the saw-mill tower.

Alone . . . and sometimes the cry of the stork
Posted on the roof, rips the silence
And then, if by chance you knocked,
I really think I would not hear.

1914

It smells of fire. For four weeks
The dry peat has burned in the marshes.
The birds forget their songs,
And the aspen tree no longer trembles.

The sun becomes
                        a punishment from God,
Fields without rain since Easter.
A one-legged man comes to the gate
And all alone cries out:

"It is coming, Apocalypse.
Fresh graves.
                    Stand by
For famine, terror, plague
And the eclipse of the stars.

But the enemy for his pleasure
Can never divide us.
                        Over our great suffering
Mary, Mother of God
Will stretch her immaculate cloak."

July 20, 1914
Slepnyovo

H.V.H.

In closeness
there is a secret boundary,
Love does not cross it.
Passion does not break it.
Nor lips
pressed together in terrible silence.
Nor the heart
torn by love.

Friendship
has no power over it.
Years of exalted happiness,
When the soul is free and full of fire,
When the flesh is innocent of languor,
have no power over it.

All who travel toward this barrier
Grow mad
All who reach it find
despair
And now you know
Why my heart, underneath your hand,
stops beating.

May, 1915
Petersburg

Somewhere there is a simple life
A transparent light, gay and warm . . .
And there, towards evening, a young girl
Talks to her neighbor behind the hedge
And only the bees
overhear their tender words.

But we live a life solemn and heavy,
Meet bitterly with bitter ceremony,
And an unfeeling wind
Disrupts our talk.

But we would exchange for nothing else
This majestic granite city of misery and glory,
These immense rivers of brilliant ice,
These enormous somber parks without sun
And the barely audible voice of the Muse.

1915

A memory
Is in me,
A white stone
At the bottom
Of a well.

I can't
Struggle with it,
I don't want to:
It is gaiety.
It is suffering.

And if someone
Looks in my eyes,
He will see it.
He'll become sad
And thoughtful
                    Like someone
Who listens to old stories.

They say the gods,
In changing men
To things,
Leave
The mind.

To give life
To my miraculous
Sadness
You have become

Memory.

Summer, 1916
Slepnyovo

from **PLANTAIN**

At my neck, small rosary beads,
My hands are hidden in a wide muff,
My eyes look out distracted
Unable to cry.

In the shadow of purpling silk
My face pales,
Straight bangs
Brush my eyebrows.

And this is nothing at all like flight,
This slow and uncertain walking
As if there were a raft under my feet
And not the squares of the parquet.

My mouth is slightly open,
My breathing difficult and uneven,
And at my shoulder flowers tremble
The flowers of an unconcluded rendezvous.

1913

When in a spirit of suicide
The people waited for our German guests,
And Byzantium's severity
Flew from the Russian church,
I heard a voice calling, consoling me,
Saying, "Come, come here,
Leave your barbarous and sinful country,
Leave Russia forever.

I will wash the blood from your hands,
I will lift the black shame from your heart,
I will cover over your sorrow.
For offenses, for defeats
                    I will find other names."
But indifferent and calm,
I stopped my ears with my hands,
I silenced the unworthy words
Come to sully a spirit sad and serene.

1917

I asked the cuckoo
"How many years
                    will I live?" . . .
The pine tops trembled,
A strip of yellow sunlight
                    fell on the grass.
But in the clear air of the thicket
No sound rang . . .
I was going back home
And a cool wind
                    touched my fevered head.

June 1, 1919

from **ANNO DOMINI MCMXXI**

You will not live again.
You will not rise from the snow
Twenty-eight holes from the bayonet
Five from the gun.

I have made a shroud for my friend,
Sad cloth.
She loves, loves blood
This Russian earth.

1921

An iron fence
A bed made of pine —
How sweet, not
To be jealous!

This bed was made
With prayers and tears;
But walk away now, go,
You are free
                And God go with you.

Now your ears won't ache
With angry words,
Now no one will burn candles
Until morning.

We have found peace,
Days filled with innocence . . .
You're crying
And I'm not worth your tears.

1921

CALUMNY

Calumny follows me everywhere.
In my sleep I hear her creeping steps
In a dead city under a steel sky
Where I hunt for my bread and a roof.
She burns in every eye
Treacherous, terrified.
She does not frighten me. I defy her.
For her I have a hard answer.
But I know what will happen.
One morning the sobs of my friends
Will trouble that sweetest sleep.
They will place an icon on my cold breast.
Then she will come in and they will not know
her.
She will mix her voice with the prayers for the
dead.
Her insatiable mouth will count out each drop of
my blood,
Each uncommitted crime.
And everyone will listen. She will vomit her
delirium
And no one will dare to look at his neighbor.
My body will rest in the trembling emptiness.
My soul, wrapped in morning's light,
will burn for the last time

With impotence, with fierce pity
For this departed world.

1921

Submit to you? You are out of your mind.
I submit only to God.
I want neither trembling nor pain.
My husband is a hangman, his house — prison.

But you understand, don't you?
I came of my own will.
December was coming, and the winds cried in the field,
And it was so bright in your slavery,
And outside the window, the dark was watching me.

So in winter weather, a bird might fly
Against sheer glass with his whole body
And blood
stain his white wing.

Now, there is happiness in me,
and I am calm.
Goodbye. You will always be dear
to me, my quiet friend
For
I was homeless, and you took me in.

1921

To lose the freshness of the words
and simplicity of feeling
Is to be a painter without sight
Or an actor without voice and hands
Or a woman
with her beauty gone.

But do not try to keep for yourself
What God gives.
We are condemned — and we understand it
well —
To give everything, to withhold nothing.

Go, alone, carry healing to the blind
And, in an hour painful with doubt,
Discover the hard malice of disciples,
The cold indifference of the mob.

1915

LOT'S WIFE

But Lot's wife looked back from
behind him, and she became a
pillar of salt.
— Genesis

The righteous followed the will of God,
An enormous opalescent light
                    on the black mountain,
But anguish called to the wife:
It is not too late, you can turn again

Toward the red towers of your native Sodom
Toward the square where you sang
                the courtyard where you walked
Toward the blind windows of the big house
Where you gave children to your beloved
    husband.

And she looked —
Chained by the pain of death
Her eyes were already blind
Her quick feet grew into the earth
Her body became transparent salt.

Who will cry for this woman?
Is she not the least of things lost?

Only I can never forget —
She who gave her life
                    for one look.

1922–24

Finally we have found a way to part,
To put out the odious flame
And, my eternal enemy, it is time
Time you learned to love someone
                                        for good.

But I, I am free. All things distract
And at night, my muse comes to console me
And glory, staggering in,
Shakes his baby rattle in my ear.

Don't bother to say prayers in my behalf
Nor, in going out, to turn back.
The black wind will calm me
The gold falling of the leaves divert me.

I accept this parting as a gift
This forgetting, as a paradise
But tell me,
          this sacrificial suffering
Will you demand it
          of someone else?

Will you dare?

REQUIEM

No, it was not under a strange sky,
Not strange wings that gave me shelter —
I was in the midst of my people,
There, where, in their misfortune, my people were.

1961

INSTEAD OF A PREFACE

In the terrible years of Yezhovism I spent seventeen months standing in line in front of the Leningrad prisons. One day someone thought he recognized me. Then, a woman with bluish lips who was behind me and to whom my name meant nothing, came out of the torpor to which we were all accustomed and said, softly (for we spoke only in whispers),

"— And that, could you describe that?"

And I said, "Yes, I can."

And then a sort of smile slid across what had been her face.

April 1, 1957
Leningrad

DEDICATION

Before this grief, mountains must bend down
And rivers stop,
But prison locks are strong,
And behind them are the labor-camp bunks
And the deadly tedium.
For others the fresh breeze is blowing,
For others the extravagant sun sets —
For us everything is the same, we know nothing,
We hear only the keys and their hateful grinding.
Only the soldiers' stiff steps.
We get up as for early Mass in the city,
The savaged city, and coming
We meet ourselves, the dead, the unbreathing.
The sun is low, the Neva misty,
It is only in the distance that hope is singing.
The sentence . . . and at once tears,
Now everything has been taken,
The rest of life, torn from her heart,
Knocked backwards by a hoodlum
And yet she walks . . . stumbles . . . alone . . .
Where are they now, unwilling friends
Of years in Hell?
What visions do they see in Siberian
    snow-storms?
What hallucinations in the circle of the moon?
I send them this goodbye and wish them well.

INTRODUCTION

This was a time, when only the dead
Smiled, glad to have peace.
And Leningrad
Swung from its prisons
Like an unused limb.
And when
Gone mad from suffering,
The condemned regiments were starting off,
And the whistles of the locomotives
Sang short songs of parting.
Over us were stars of death,
And innocent Russia
Struggled under the bloodied boot,
And the tires of the Black Maria.

March, 1940

I

They took you away at daybreak,
And I, as though following a corpse, came out.
In the dark room, the children wept,
In God's corner, the candle guttered.
Your lips held the cold of an icon,
I won't forget the deathly sweat on your
forehead.
I will go like the wives of the Streltzy dead
And howl under the towers of the Kremlin.

1935

II

The silent Don flows silently,
The yellow moon comes into the house,

Comes in with cap askew,
And the yellow moon sees a ghost

A woman sick
A woman alone

Husband in the grave, son in prison . . .
Say one prayer for me.

III

No, this is not I,
But someone else,
For this much
I could not suffer,
Let the black cloth
Cover
What has happened
And let them take away
The lanterns . . .
                Night.

IV

If you could have seen, mocker,
Beloved and spoiled of all your friends,
Happy sinner of Tsarskoe Selo
What was to be your life:
How with packages, and three hundredth in line
You would stand under the Crosses,
Your tears burning a hole
In the New Year's ice —
Where the prison's poplar swings and bends
And there is no sound — and where how many
Innocent lives end . . .

V

For seventeen months I cried,
I called you to come home.
And I threw myself at the feet of the hangmen
For you, my terror,
My son.
Everything is entangled forever,
I can no longer tell
Which is beast
Which man.
For how long will we wait the judgment?
And there are only
Dusty flowers
The clanging of censers
And here and there,
                                        clues to nowhere,
And, eyeing me straight in the eye,
Terrorizing me with imminent death,
One huge star.

VI

The light weeks fly,
And I do not understand what has happened —
How for you, my darling son
The white night looked into the jail
And will look again
With the hot eye of a hawk
And speak to you
Of your high cross, and of death.

1939

VII

THE SENTENCE

And the word fell as a rock
On my living breast.
No matter, I am ready, am I not?
Somehow, I will cope.

I have much to do:
I must kill my memories
                    down to the last one,
I must change my soul into stone,
I must learn to live again.

Otherwise
            there is the hot rustling of summer
As if there were a festival, beyond my window.
Long ago I knew of this
This translucent day, and the emptied house.

Summer, 1939

VIII

TO DEATH

Since you come anyway, why not now?
I am waiting for you — my life is difficult.
I blow out the light and open the door for you.
How simple you are, what a miracle!
Take any mask you like,
Burst in as a poisoned shell
Or come cautiously, as a proficient thief,
Or with the delirium of typhus fever.
Or come as the legend you yourself invented
And we have heard till we are sick:
Let me see the top of the blue cap
And the house-manager pale with fear.
To me now, it is all the same.
The Yenisey turns, the North Star shines,
And the dark blue radiance of his eyes
Is covered by the final terror.

August 19, 1939
Fountain House

IX

Already madness with her wing
Covers half my soul,
Offers me her fiery wine,
Calls me to the black valley.

And I understand. I must
Give madness the victory,
Must listen to my own
Raving, as if it came from someone else.

And madness will not let me
Bring away anything — only myself
(However much I beg
However much I trouble her with pleading):

Not bring the terrible eye of my son —
Suffering made stone —
Not bring the day when the storm first came
Not the hour of meeting at the prison,

Not the charity of a cool hand,
Not the uneasy shade of the linden,
Not the sound, small and distant,
Of the last words of consolation.

May 4, 1940
Fountain House

X

CRUCIFIXION

"Do not weep for me, Mother,
In the tomb, I exist."

The great hour was glorified
by the angels' choir,
The sky was melted
in a fire.
He said to the Father, "Why have you
abandoned me?"
And to the Mother, "Do not weep for me."

Mary Magdalene struggled and sobbed,
The best-loved disciple was turned to rock
But there where the silent Mother stood,
There, no one dared to look.

1940–43

EPILOGUE

I

I found out how faces wilt
How beneath eyelids fear looks out
How suffering cheeks become stiff pages of
    cuneiform
How black hair
Is suddenly made ashen.
And how, on submissive lips, smiles wither
And fright trembles in a small dry laugh.
And I do not pray for myself only
But for all who stood with me
In the fierce cold and in July's white heat,
Under the red unseeing wall.

II

The day of remembering comes again.
I see, I hear, I sense them:

She who drags it out to the end,
And she who, born Russian, no longer walks this
Russian land,

And she who shakes her beautiful head,
"I am coming here as to my home," she says.

I would like to call them each by name,
But they have taken away the list — and where
will I find one?

For them I have woven a wide shroud
Out of their misery, out of their overheard
words.

Any place and at all times, I remember them,
Even in my new distress I do not forget them,

And if they gag my exhausted throat
Out of which one hundred million people shout,

Let them pray for me in some way
On the eve of my own death day.

And if sometime in this country
They decide to make a monument to me,

To this honor I will give consent,
But only with this condition — that they do not
put it

Either by the sea where I was born
(That sea with whom my last ties are broken),

Nor in the Tsar's Park by the sacred willow tree
Where that inconsolable phantom looks for me,

But here where I stood three hundred hours,
Here, where they would not unlock the door.

Even in happy death, I would remember
The Black Maria's thunder,

The hateful door banged shut, and the howl
Of the old woman, like the howl of a wounded
animal.

And from immobile eyelids of bronze,
Let the melted snow slide like tears,

And the doves of the prison call in the distance,
And the boats of the Neva go by in silence.

March, 1940

from **REED**

WILLOW

And I grew up in patterned tranquility
In a cool children's room in the young century.
And human voices did not please me,
But the voice of the wind, I understood.
And I loved burrs and nettles
But more than anything, I loved the silver
    willow.
And, grateful, he lived
All his life with me, and with his weeping
    branches
Fanned my sleeplessness with dreams.
— How odd it is! I have outlived him.
There the stump stands, and the alien voices
Of other willows speak of this and that
Under our old skies.
But I grow quiet
        as when a brother dies.

1940

MISCELLANEOUS POEMS 1940–1942

TO THE PEOPLE OF LONDON

Time, with an indifferent pen,
Writes out the twenty-fourth play of
Shakespeare.
And we, seated at this horrible feast,
Read of Hamlet, of Caesar and of Lear
Over a river of lead;
And it would be better if today
With psalms and torches
We followed the casket of young Juliet
Or looked at Macbeth's window
And trembled with the killer —
But not this, not this, not this,
This by now we have no strength to read!

1940

TO THE MEMORY OF MY LITTLE NEIGHBOR IN LENINGRAD, VALIA SMIRNOV

I

They have dug trenches in the garden
And the lights are out.
O Petersburg orphans,
O my children!
Under the earth, we breathe badly,
Pain beats in our ears,
Above the whistling of the shell
We hear the crying of the child.

II

Knock with your little fist and I will open.
I have always opened my door.
I am far away now, beyond the high mountain,
Beyond the desert, beyond the wind and the heat
But I will never abandon you . . .

. . . .

I haven't heard your last cry.
You haven't asked for your bread.
Bring me, then, a little branch of maple
Or several stems of green grass,
Like those you brought last spring.

Bring me a little water in your hand,
Pure cold water from our Neva,
And from your small gold head
I will wash all trace of blood.

April 23, 1942

POEM WITHOUT A HERO

Triptych
1940–1962

Leningrad-Tashkent-Moscow

Di rider finirai
Pria dell'aurora
Don Giovanni

Deus conservat omnia
(Motto on the coat-of-arms
of the house I was living in,
when I started to write the poem)

INSTEAD OF A PREFACE

> Some are dead, some far away . . .
> Pushkin

During the previous autumn she had sent a messenger: a fragment of the work. But she came to me for the first time at the Fountain House on the night of December 27, 1940. I hadn't called her. And, that dark cold day of my last winter in Leningrad, I hardly expected her.

Her arrival was preceded by some trivial incidents of so little importance that I don't feel I can call them "events."

That night I wrote two fragments of the first part ("1913" and the "Dedication"). Early in June, almost without intending to, I wrote "The Other Side of the Coin." Then in Tashkent (in two sessions) I wrote "Epilogue," which thus became the poem's third part; and I made substantial additions to parts one and two.

I dedicate this poem to the memory of those who heard it first, my friends and fellow-citizens who died in Leningrad during the seige.

When I read this poem aloud I remember them, I hear their voices, and for me it is this hidden chorus that will always justify this work.

April 8, 1943

Often voices come to me with upsidedown and absurd interpretations of *Poem Without a Hero.* And there are always those who advise me to make the poem less obscure.

I won't do that.

Poem Without a Hero doesn't have any third, seventh or twenty-ninth meaning.

I don't want to change it or clarify it.

"What's written's written."

November, 1944. Leningrad

DEDICATION

In memory of Vs. K.

. . . .

. . . but now I am short of paper
I write on your rough drafts
And another's word shines through
And, as it was once
a snowflake held in the hand,
Trusting and without regret melts
And the dark eyebrows of Antinous
Rise suddenly, and green mist
The swell of familiar breezes . . .
Is it the sea? No, branches of evergreen
Spread like carpets of sea-foam.
Always closer, closer . . .
Marche Funèbre
Chopin . . .

December 27, 1940. Night. Fountain House

SECOND DEDICATION

To O.A.G.–S.

Is it you, Psyche-Confusionaria,
Here in the air over me
Waving a white and black fan,
Bending furtively in order to say
That you have already crossed Lethe
And breathe another spring?
Don't tell me about it
I hear it for myself:
In the lukewarm rain stuttering on the roof
In the continual whispering of the ivy.
Someone small is getting ready to live.
He is green, feathery, trying hard —
Tomorrow he will show off his new cloak.
I sleep:
Above me, only...
"Spring," they call her,
I call her "solitude."
I sleep:
In my dream I see our young life:
The cup that passed *him* by
I will give you openly

As a souvenir;
As if it were a pure flame in the clay,
Or a snowdrop in a mass grave.

May 25, 1945. Fountain House

THE THIRD AND LAST

Once on Epiphany Eve...
Zhukovsky

Enough of this cold terror!
I will call up the Bach Chaconne
And behind it the man
Who will not become my dear husband,
But he and I will do such things
As will shock this twentieth century.
By accident I accepted him
As one given in secret
To share a bitter destiny.
It will be late
When he comes to me
To drink the New Year's wine
At the Palace of Fountains.
And he'll remember the Eve of Epiphany,
The maple tree through the window, the
nuptial candles
And the poem's mortal flight...
But not the first branch of lilac,
Not the ring, not the sweet prayers —
He is coming
And with him...
Death.

1956. January 5 (le jour des Rois)

INTRODUCTION

FROM NINETEEN-FORTY,
AS FROM A TOWER, I SEE EVERYTHING
AS IF I SAID GOODBYE TO ALL
AS I SAID GOODBYE BEFORE
AS IF HAVING MADE THE SIGN
OF THE CROSS
I WENT DOWN UNDER DARK
VAULTS.

August 25, 1941. Leningrad under seige

PART ONE
NINETEEN THIRTEEN
PETERSBURG STORY
CHAPTER ONE

Sumptuous, the New Year's
feast stretches out,
The stems of its roses are
wet . . .

Rosary, 1914

Unlike Tatyana, we never make
predictions.

Pushkin

In my hot youth — when
George the Third was
king . . .

Don Juan

New Year's Eve. The Fountain House. The author sees, instead of the person she is waiting for, ghosts from 1913. They wear masks. The white mirror room. Lyric digression: "The Guest of the Future." *Masked ball. The poet. The ghosts.*

To make the evening shine
  I light the candles I love so much,
    And here with you, you who haven't come,
      I celebrate the arrival of nineteen-forty.
But . . .
  God's strength be with us!
    The flame in the glass is gone,
      "And the wine burns like poison."
Burst of bitter dialogue
  When the incubi are resurrected
    And the clock's not struck . . .
This anguish has no measure,
  I stand on the threshold, myself a ghost,
    Standing guard over my last comfort.
I hear the long ring at the door,
  I feel the damp rise, I turn to stone,
    I grow cold, I burn . . .
And, as if I'd remembered something,
  I turn half away,
    I say in a low voice:

"You're wrong: the doges' Venice
Is here right now . . . but masks,
Mantles, sceptres, crowns —
Today they should be left in the anteroom.
Just now the idea came to me: I ought to honor
The libertines. The libertines of the New Year!"
This is Faust, this, Don Giovanni,
Dapertutto, Jokannon;
And the most modest is the northerner Glahn
Or the murderer, Dorian,
And to their Dianas
All whisper the lesson.
And someone else with tympani
Drags in a goat-footed one.
For them the walls open up,
The lights flash, the sirens howl
And the ceiling swells like a dome.
Not that I'm afraid to be in the public view . . .
Hamlet's garter is nothing to me,
Nor the undulations of Salome,
Nor the step of the Man in the Iron Mask,
I am harder than that . . .
Whose turn is it now to be terrorized,
To draw back, to go away, to give up,
To ask to be forgiven for an old sin?

It's clear:
Not to me, but to . . . ?
The supper's not spread for them
And my path's not for them.
He has hidden the tail under the folds of the
evening coat . . .
So that he limps slightly, but what
elegance . . .
But
You wouldn't dare
Bring here
The Prince of Darkness?
Mask, skull, face —
Only Goya dared express it,
This malicious suffering.
Jester, darling of all,
To him the most foul sinner is
The re-incarnation of grace . . .

Let him who is merry be merry,
But how is it that I, of all of them —
That I alone am alive?
Tomorrow the morning will wake me,
And no one will judge me,
Beyond the window
The blue daylight will laugh;
But I'm afraid: I'll go in alone,
Without taking off my silk shawl,

I'll smile at everyone and keep still.
And she who used to wear black agates
And was first in the valley of Jehoshaphat
I don't want to see her again . . .
Are not the last days at hand? . . .
I've forgotten your lessons,
Gas bags and false prophets! —
But you don't forget me.
As the future ripens in the past,
So the past rots in the future —
A procession of dead leaves.

W *On the shining parquet, a sound of steps,*
H *Of those who are not here.*
I *The blue smoke of a cigar.*
T *And in all the mirrors*
E *The one who doesn't appear*
The one who can't enter this room.
He's no better and no worse than the others,
R *But he does not breathe in*
O *the cold hard frost of Lethe,*
O *And his hand is warm.*
M *Guest from the future! — Can it be then*
That he comes to me,
Turning left at the bridge?

. . . Even as a child I was terrified of
masquerades,

It always seemed to me
That some extra shadow
"Without face or name" moved
Among the maskers . . .
But let's begin the feast
The solemn feast of the New Year!
That Hoffmannesque midnight
I'm not going to publicize it
And I will ask the others . . .
But wait!
It seems you're not on the lists
With Cagliostri, Magi, Messalinas,
Dressed up in zebra stripes,
Crudely painted in bright colors —
You . . .
contemporary of the oak of Mamre,
Age-old interlocutor of the moon.
You . . . who won't be moved by false outcries,
They ought to learn from you,
The Hammurabis, the Lycurgeses, the
Solons.
He is an eccentric.
He doesn't wait until gout and honour
Pin him
To a sumptuous jubilee chair.
He carries his victory among the
heather in flower
Through the desert wilderness.
And he's guilty of nothing: not this,

Not that, not some third thing . . .
in general, sins
Do not attach themselves to poets.
To dance before the Ark of the Covenant
To disappear! . . .
Never mind! This —
Poetry said it better.
We only dream the cock's cry:
Outside the window
The endless night, the steaming Neva
And on and on, devilry
In the City of Peter . . .
No stars in the narrow windows,
The end must be already here,
But the chatter of the masquerade
Is carefree, thoughtless, without
shame . . .
A shout:
"Hero on stage!"
Don't worry, he'll soon take the place
Of this great hulking fool
And will sing the sacred vendetta . . .
But why do you all slip away together
As if a bride had been found for each,
Leaving me eye to eye
With a black picture frame in the dark
And looking out of it that hour,

Of all dramas most bitter —
And not yet wept for?

All this doesn't come to the surface at once.
I hear it whispered
Like a musical phrase. "Goodbye! It's time!
I leave you alive
But you will be my *widow*
You — dove, sunlight, sister!"
On the landing two joined shadows . . .
Then — from the bottom stair
A shout: "Don't do it!" — and in the distance
A clear voice:
"I am ready to die."

The torches go out, the ceiling moves lower. The white room becomes again the author's room. Words from the dark:

Death doesn't exist — we all know it,
There's no comfort in repeating it,
But what does exist — let them tell me.
Who's knocking?
. . . Everybody has come in . . .
Is it the guest from beyond the mirror? Or
Something sudden
Like lightning at the window . . .

His forehead is pale, his eyes open . . .
   Are they so fragile, then, the gravestones,
      Is granite softer than wax . . .
Absurd, absurd, absurd! — And for this absurdity
   I'll soon be white-haired
      I will become someone else.
Why do you summon me with your hand?

For one moment of peace
I would give up eternal peace.

ACROSS THE STAIRCASE LANDING INTERMEZZO

Right beside that passage (" . . . and the chatter of the masquerade is carefree, thoughtless, without shame . . . ") such lines as the following shake and flutter, but I have not admitted them to the main text:

"Let me assure you, it's nothing new . . .
Signor Casanova, you're a child . . . "
"At St. Isaac's exactly at six . . . "
"We'll get there somehow in the dark,
From here to 'the Dog' " . . .
"And you where?"
— "God knows!"
The Sancho Panzas and the Don Quixotes
And, unfortunately, Sodom's Lots
Drink the poisonous juice.
The Aphrodites come out of the foam,
The Helens move at the window,
The hour of madness comes closer.
And once again from the grotto of the Fountains,
Where an amorous torpor cools to ice,
A certain red-headed and hairy man
Drags the Satyress
Through the ghostly door.
More elegant than all and higher,
Although it does not see and does not hear —

Does not curse, pray, or breathe,
The head of Madame de Lamballe,
And beautiful, playful, enterprising
You who dance the goat-like Chechetka,
Once again humble and mild, coo
"Que me veut mon Prince Carnaval?"

And at the same time from the depths of the room, from the stage, from the inferno or from the top of the Goethian Brocken, she *appears (but perhaps it is her ghost):*

The little ankle boots knock like hooves,
Earrings clatter like tiny cymbals,
Treacherous horns pierce the pale curls,
She's drunk with the evil dance, —
As if from a vase of black figures
She runs toward the blue wave
Nude and elegant.
And after her in overcoat and helmet
You come, without a mask,
Ivanushka of the ancient fairytale —
What tortures you today, Ivanushka?
How much rancor in every word,
What dark places in your love —
But why does this streak of blood
Twist the petal of your cheeks?

CHAPTER TWO

> Can you see him at your knees
> The one who left your prison for white death?
>
> 1913

The heroine's bedroom. A candle burns. Over the bed three portraits of the mistress in her stage-roles, to the right as the Satyress, in the middle as Confusionaria, to the left — a portrait in shadows. It may be Columbine, or so it seems to me. To others it seems Donna Anna (of the "Steps of the Commander"). Through the mansard window we see young blacks playing with snowballs. A blizzard. New Year's Eve. The Confusionaria stirs, comes down out of the painting, and it seems to her that she hears a voice read:

The little satin-lined fur coat whips open!
  Don't be angry, Columba,
    If I touch lips to this cup, too:
      I am punishing myself, not you.
All the same, the time to pay is coming nearer —
  Through the fine dust of the blizzard
    You can see Meyerhold's black boys
      Making an uproar.
And all around the city of Peter,
  That old city that broke the people's backs

(As the people said at the time) —
Convoys of grain, horses' manes, harnesses
Daubed up with roses
And under a cloud of black wings.
But now she comes, faking a smile,
Flies on to Mariinsky's stage, the Prima
Our ineffable swan —
And a late-coming snob cracks jokes.
The orchestra seems to be playing from another
world
(Out of nowhere a phantom whirls)
And — is it a presentiment of sunrise? —
Along the line of people, a shiver of fever
passes.
And again that voice, familiar
Almost an echo of mountain thunder —
Our triumph and glory!
It fills our hearts with shudderings
Skims over the non-roads
Of the country that fed it.
Snow, blue-white on the branches . . .
The corridor at the Colleges of Peter
Straight, endless, with roaring echoes
(Whatever happens becomes a stubborn dream
In anyone
Who passes there)
But the answer is close enough to make you
laugh;

From behind the screen the mask of Petrushka,
Around the bonfires the coachman's dance,
Above the palace the black and yellow
banner flying . . .
Each is in his appointed place,
The Summer Garden breathes out a hint
Of the fifth act . . . and from the hell of
Tsushima
Still another ghost. A drunken sailor
sings . . .
Bobsleds tinkle like a parade,
The goaty blanket drags behind . . .
Pass by, ghosts! He is there, alone.
On the wall is his hard profile.
Oh beauty, is Gabriel or Mephistopheles
Your champion?
The demon himself with Tamara's smile,
But what witchcraft is hidden
In that terrifying smoky face —
Flesh becoming soul,
Over the ear an antique curl —
And about the messenger, everything —
enigma.
Was it all a dream,
Or did he send into the crowded room
A wine glass with a black rose?
His glance and his heart are dead.
Did he elbow his way in here in order to meet

the Commander
In his already-damned house?
And his words revealed
How you were in a new space,
As if outside of time, —
In crystal poles,
In splendors of amber
There, at the mouth of Lethe — of the
Neva.
You have run here from the portrait,
And on the wall the empty picture frame
Waits until morning.
It's your turn to dance without a partner!
And I'm willing to take the part
Of the fatal chorus.

You have red spots on your cheeks,
You ought to climb back on the canvas;
Tonight in fact is the night
That the bill must be paid . . .
But for me this opium-sleepiness
Is more difficult to conquer than death itself.

You have come to Russia out of nowhere,
My blond marvel,
Columbine of the 1910s!
Why the veiled and hawkish stare,
Petersburg doll, little actress,

You — one of my doubles.
We must add this title, too.
Oh friend of poets,
I, heiress to your glory,
Here, in the shade of the cedar tree of
Kellomiage
To that music in magic metres,
The furious wind of Leningrad,
See a dance of courtly bones . . .
The wedding candles melt,
Under the veil "the kissable shoulders,"
The church thunders with "Enter, dove!"
Mountains of Parma violets in April —
And the rendezvous in the Malta Chapel
A curse in your heart.
A vision of the golden age
Or a black crime
From the fearful chaos of the past?
At least tell me now:
is it possible
That once you really were alive
And that you stamped the pavement of the
squares
With your dazzling little foot? . . .

The house is more gayly colored
Than a strolling player's cart,
Peeling cupids guard the altar of Venus.

You haven't put singing birds in the cage,
You have furnished the bedroom as a bower,
The merry skobar
Won't recognize the rustic lover.
Hidden in the walls a winding staircase,
On the azure walls, the saints —
Blessings half-stolen . . .
You received your friends stretched out in bed
All in flowers, like Botticelli's "Spring,"
And the dragoon-Pierrot suffered —
And wore a certain smile: "victim of the
evening,"
Of all who loved you he was the most
superstitious,
And you were magnet to his steel;
When they offer you roses
He grows pale, studies through tears
The fame of his rival.
I have not seen your husband,
I, frost pasted to the window . . .
Listen! The hours strike on the fortress
clock . . .
I don't mark the houses with crosses,
You can come to me without being afraid —
Your horoscope has been ready for some time . . .

CHAPTER THREE

We'll meet again at Petersburg,
As if we had buried the sun there.
Osip Mandelstam

It was last year . . .
M. Lozinsky

And under the arch of Galernaya Street . . .
1913

Petersburg, 1913. Lyric digression: last memories of Tsarskoe Selo. The wind, as if prophesying or remembering, speaks:

Christmas celebrations warmed by bonfires,
The carriages pell mell down the bridges,
The city, in mourning, sailed
Toward some unknown destination,
Sometimes with the Neva,
Sometimes against the Neva,
But in any case away from its own tombs.
The arch stood black in Galernaya Street,
In the Summer Garden, the weathercock rang out,
And over the silver age
The silver moon cooled to ice.

Because through every street,
  Because at every door,
    Slowly, the shadow drew closer,
The wind tore posters from the wall,
  Smoke danced the hopak on the roof,
    And the lilac smelled of cemeteries.
And cursed by the Tsarina Avdotya,
  With Dostoevsky the bedeviled city
    Receded in its own mists.
And once again the debauched old Petersburger
  Ogled out of the dark,
    The drum rolled as if for an execution . . .
And all the time in that cold stuffiness,
  Threatening, pre-war, lascivious,
    An incomprehensible reverberation hid
      itself;
In those days we heard it mutedly,
  It hardly reached us
    And quickly drowned in the piled snow on
      the Neva.
As if in the mirror of a terrible night,
  Man raves
    And will not recognize himself.
But along the Neva's legendary esplanade,
  The Twentieth Century approached —
    Not the one on the calendar, the real one.

And I must get home quickly
Down the Cameron Gallery
To the mysterious garden of ice
Of silent waterfalls
Where the Nine are satisfied with me
As you were once.
And beyond the island, beyond the garden
Won't they meet again
Just as they were
        The glances of our clear eyes?
And then won't you say
        One more time
That word that overcomes death
And unties the enigma of my life?

FOURTH AND LAST

Love passed, and the face of death
Came clear
and nearer

Vs. K.

A corner of the Field of Mars. A house built at the beginning of the nineteenth century by the Adamini brothers, a house that in 1942 took a direct hit during an air raid. A high bonfire burns. The bells of the Saviour of the Blood are tolling. In a field beyond the blizzard the apparition of a court ball. In an interval between the sounds, the silence itself speaks:

Who's there under the dark windows numbed
with cold,
Who carries "the blond lock" in his heart,
Who looks into the gloom?
"Help! It's not too late.
But you are cold
And alien, night!"
A wind full of Baltic saltiness,
A dance of snow-squalls on the Field of Mars.
Invisible hooves ring out,
An endless anguish
In him who has only a little time to live,
Who asks nothing of God but death

And who will be forgotten forever.
He's been walking back and forth under the
window,
The beam from the corner lamppost,
Implacable and opaque,
Is fixed on him.
He has waited since midnight.
But he has finished waiting. The graceful
masquer
Back on the "Road to Damascus"
Returns . . . and not alone.
With her somebody "without face or
name" . . .
An unambiguous goodbye
Through the slanted flames of the bonfire.
He has seen everything — the palaces
collapse . . .
And in response the shattered sob:
"You, Columbine, sunlight, sister!
I leave you alive,
But you will be *my* widow,
And now . . .
Goodbye!"
On the landing the smell of perfume,
And the dragoons' cornet — with poems,
With senseless death in his heart —
Will sound out, if he finds the courage . . .
In order to glorify you

He squanders the final moment.
Look:
He's not in the bitter marshes of the Masure,
Not on the blue Carpathian Peaks . . .
He's stretched across your door!
May God pardon you!
The poet has to die many times,
Foolish child: he himself chose this way —
He couldn't bear the first outrage,
He didn't know at what door he stood,
He didn't understand what kind of road
Would open up before him . . .

Here I am — your old conscience —
I discovered the charred manuscript
And on the corner of the windowsill
In the dead man's house
I put it down —
And on tiptoe went away . . .

AFTERWORD

EVERYTHING'S READY: THE POEM
AS IS ITS WAY, IS SILENT.
BUT SUDDENLY THE THEME BREAKS
    OUT,
HAMMERS AT THE WINDOW LIKE A FIST,
AND FROM FAR OFF
A TERRIBLE SOUND
        WILL ANSWER THIS CHALLENGE —
GURGLINGS, MOANS, SHRIEKS —
AND THE APPARITION OF CROSSED
    HANDS . . .

1940–1962

SECOND PART
INTERMEZZO
THE OTHER SIDE OF THE COIN

I drink the waters of Lethe,
My doctor objects to low spirits.
Pushkin

In my beginning is my end.
(motto of Mary, Queen of Scots)

Scene of the action: the Fountain House, January 5, 1941. Through the window, a ghostly maple covered with snow. Just now the Hell's Harlequinade of 1913, having waked from silence the great "Epoch of Silence," disappeared. It has left behind the usual disorder of a long cortège, whether of celebration or of funeral: torch smoke, flowers on the floor, the eternally-lost sacred souvenirs.

The wind howls in the chimney, and in the howl you can just make out a few snatches of Requiem. *As to what the mirrors reflect, never mind.*

. . . the jasmine grove
Where Dante walked and the air is empty.
N.K.

I

My editor didn't like it much,
He swore he was overworked and sick,
He got an unlisted phone
And he complained: "Three subjects at once!
I mean, look at the last line,
Who loves whom, who knows?

II

Rendezvous — but with whom, when, why?
Who was killed, who's still alive?
Who wrote it and who's the hero
And anyway. at a time like this
Who cares about discussions of 'the poet'
Or the swarming of spirits?"

III

I told him, "There were three of them —
The principal one dressed as a milepost,
Another in devil's weeds —
And these two are to be handed down the
centuries.
Their verses worked it out for them . . .
But the third scarcely lived twenty years.

IV

I'm sorry for him" . . . And once more
Word falls against word,
The music box thunders,
And on the small chipped phial
A twisted, angry tongue of flame,
An unfamiliar poison, burns.

V

And I always dream
That for *** I'm writing a libretto
And the music won't let me go.
And any dream has a life of its own,
A Blue Bird, a soft embalmer,
A castle platform at Elsinore.

VI

And I was not satisfied,
I had always hoped that the far-away shout
Of the infernal harlequinade
Would burst like a puff of smoke
Past the white room
And be swept away through dark pines.

VII

That stack of ramshackle junk,
We can't get rid of it.

That old Cagliostro does weird things,
He's a most elegant devil,
But he won't cry with me over death
And he doesn't know what conscience is.

VIII

Midnight. No hint of Roman Carnival.
The melody of the Cherubinic
Trembles at the closed porch of the church.
Nobody knocks at my door,
Only dream: of mirrors in mirrors, of silence
Standing guard over silence.

IX

And with me is My Seventh
Half-dead, dumb,
The mouth crooked and slack,
Like the mouth of a tragic mask.
It's smeared with black paint
And filled with dry dirt.

X

. . . .
. . . .
. . . .
. . . .
. . . .
. . . .

XI

. . . .

. . . .

. . . .

And so the decades file by, torture,
Deportations, executions. Sing —
You see . . .
I can't

[And especially if I dream
Of that inevitable next thing:
Death everywhere — the city in flames,
And Tashkent wearing flowers like a bride . . .
There soon the winds from Asia
Will tell me
what it is that matters,
what it is that lasts.]

XII

Squander myself in an official hymn?
Not for me, not for me, not for me
The diadem they take off when you die.
I will need my lyre,
The lyre of Sophocles, not Shakespeare.
For Destiny stands at the door.

XIII

And a subject like that!
A crushed chrysanthemum
After the funeral has passed!
And between 'think of' and 'think up' —
The distance from Luga
To the country of the Satin Domino.

XIV

The devil's work:
                                        I went through that trunk
But why is everything my fault?
And I'm so quiet, so simple,
Plantain, White Flock . . .
                                                        Make excuses?
How, my friends?

XV

Know this: they will accuse you of plagiarism.
Am I guiltier than the rest?
It's all so unimportant.
I admit the fiasco, admit I failed —
I don't deny being upset, in fact
The casket has a triple bottom.

XVI

I confess it, I made use
Of invisible ink
And of script you read in a mirror.
It was the only road there was —
Finding it was a miracle
And I am in no hurry to step off.

XVII

Someone would come from an earlier age
Hailed out of an intimate dream of El Greco's,
He would say nothing, make me understand
With the summer's smile
In his time I'd have been about as acceptable
As the seven deadly sins.

XVIII

And now from some coming century
The eyes of someone I never met.
He would fix me with a bold stare
And hold out toward my disappearing shadow
An armful of wet lilacs
From some time when the storm will have
passed.

XIX

But the seductive centenarian
Suddenly comes to herself,
She is ready to play.
I'm not the guilty one.
She drops a lace handkerchief,
Half-closes her eyes — eyelids heavy with
poems,
A temptress with Bryullovian shoulders.

XX

I drank her drop by drop
Obsessed by a black diabolical thirst
And couldn't rid myself
Of that possessed woman:
I threatened her with the Star Chamber,
I drove her to her native garret —

[— To the dark, under the pines of Manfred,
To the shore where the dead Shelley lay
Looking straight into the clouds, —
And all the skylarks in the world
Shredded the abyss of ether,
And George Gordon held the torch.]

XXI

But she says over and over, stubbornly,
"I'm certainly not that English lady,
I am not, in fact, Clara Gazul,
I have no genealogy
Or perhaps — a solar and fabulous one.
July itself brings me here.

XXII

But your ambiguous glory
Which lay for twenty years in the ditch,
I will serve it in another style.
We will feast together, you and I,
And with a royal kiss
I will reward your bitter midnight."

January 3–5, 1941
The Fountain House and Tashkent

PART THREE
EPILOGUE

I love you, creature of Peter!
Bronze Horseman

That place is to be laid waste. . . .
* * *

And the mute deserted squares
Where before sunrise they held executions.
Annensky

The white night of June 24, 1942. The city is covered with rubble. You can see everything from the Maritime Station to Smolny as if it were on the palm of your hand. Here and there some remaining fires are burning themselves out. In Sheremetev Garden the lime trees are in flower and the nightingale sings. Outside a knocked-out third floor window a mutilated maple stands, and beyond the maple a black emptiness stretches away. The big guns boom off toward Kronstadt, but in general, things are quiet. The author, 7,000 kilometers away, speaks out:

To my city

Below the roof of The Fountain House
With a lamp and a ring of keys
An evening laziness moves,
And the far-off echo of shouts
Disturbs with inappropriate laughter
The profound lethargy of things.
And witness to every event,
In the early morning and at nightfall,
The old maple looks into the room
And knowing that we must separate,
As if asking for help, holds out
A black withered hand.
The land shuddered underfoot,
And a certain star looked into
My still-lived-in house
And waited for the signal agreed on . . .
It must be there — at Tobruk,
It must be here — around the corner.
You, dark auditor of bright delirium,
You who are neither the first nor the last,
What do you have ready for me?
You won't drink this bitterness,
You bring it just to the lips,
This bitterness of the lower depths —
This news of our separation!
No, don't touch my head with your hand —

On the watch you gave me
Time stops forever.
Disaster. Our fates are set.
And in woods destroyed by fire
The cuckoo has stopped singing.

And behind barbed wire
In the heart of the dense Taiga —
For how long now —
Having become a handful of camp dust,
A fairy tale from the terrible past,
My double goes to the interrogation,
And then comes from the interrogation,
Two messengers from the noseless Girl
Escort him.
And even at this distance —
Is it not a miracle! —
I can hear the sound of my own voice:
I've paid for you
with ready money,
For exactly ten years I walked
under the whip,
I looked
neither to the left nor the right
And a bad reputation
rustled behind me.

And when you did not become my tomb,

You, granite-like, satanic, kind,
You turned pale, became dead and silent.
Our separation is a lie:
I can never be separated from you,
My shadow is on your walls,
My image is in your canals,
The sound of my steps is in the rooms of the
    Hermitage,
Where I walked with my friend,
And in the old Volkovo Field
Where I could weep freely
Above the silent communal graves.
And what has been noted in the first part
Of love, of passion, of betrayal,
Free verse has thrown down from her wings.
My city stands "sewed up" . . .
The grave-stones weigh heavily
Over your unsleeping eyes.
But it seems as if you follow me,
You who stayed to die
In brightness of steeples,
                    in brightness of water.
You were waiting for messengers . . .
Above you the round dance
Of the temptresses, your white nights.
A happy phrase — "at home" —
And now unknown to anyone,
Everybody looks through another man's
    windows.

Here in Tashkent, there in New York,
The air in exile is bitter
Like poisoned wine.
Which of you would not have admired me,
When in the flying fish's belly
I saved myself from the evil hunt,
Running through woods full of dangerous
Enemies, like a woman possessed of devils
As she flew over Brocken at night.

. . . .

And then up ahead
The Kama cooled and hardened,
And someone said, "Quo vadis?"
But before I could move my lips
The crazy Urals thundered
With tunnels and bridges.
And the road opened out,
That funereal road that comes at last
To the crystal silence
Of the Siberian plains.
Too many have already walked over it,
Over it they took my son.
And now, with the cold fear of death
With minds fixed on the time of revenge
With dry eyes turned to the ground
With tight and nervous hands
Ahead of me, out of a country turned to dust
All Russia walked, toward the East.

Finished in Tashkent, August 18, 1942

MISCELLANEOUS POEMS 1943–1946

Wild honey smells of freedom
The dust — of sunlight
The mouth of a young girl, like a violet
But gold — smells of nothing.

Mignonette smells of water
Love smells of apples
And now we know
Blood smells of blood.

To the mob's dismal cry
The Roman governor
Washes his hands in vain
And under the stifling shadows
Of the royal house
In vain the Scots queen
With tight hands
Scours the red spots.

1943

THREE AUTUMNS

I do not feel the smiles of summer,
I have not found mystery in winter,
But I am certain I have known
Three autumns in each year.

The first, a festival in disorder
Teasing yesterday's summer,
Leaves fly like tatters from old notebooks,
Haze carries the odor of incense.
Everything is sweet, lacy, luminous.

The birch trees are the first
                    to enter the dance
To wear transparent cloaks
To shake their transient tears
Over the neighbor's fence.

But we are only at the beginning of the story.
In a second, in a minute, another
Autumn, impassable as conscience,
Sinister as an aerial assault.

Suddenly everything seems older, pale,
Summer's sweetness is pillaged,
The clang of gold trumpets

Drifts in fog . . .

Cold clouds of incense
Hide the height of the sky,
A burst of wind
                    and everything opens.
We understand. The drama is over,
This is not the third autumn.
                    This is death.

1943, Tashkent

Now my loved souls are with the stars.
How sweet, to have no one to lose;
To be able to cry. And the air at Tsarskoe Selo
Was made for lines of verse.

The pond's silver willow
Sweeps September's brilliant water
And rising from those other days, silent,
My own ghost confronts me.

Many lyres hang from these trees,
But for mine, too, there's a place.
Thin rain splashed with sun
Is a message and a consolation.

1944

"LENINGRAD ELEGY"

This rude century
Turned me aside like a river
And this unintended life
Flows in new channels
Past strange banks.
What landscapes have I missed?
What curtains rose and fell
Without me? What friends
Did I never meet?
What skylines not see
That might have brought my tears?
I know only this one city,
I could find it by touch in my sleep . . .
How many poems did I not write?
They hang in the air around me, a weird choir,
And some day
May suffocate me . . .
I knew beginnings and ends
And life after the end, and something else,
Something I must no longer think about . . .
An ordinary woman
Took my unique place
Used my real name
Left me a pseudonym

With it I do
                    what I can.
Terrible! It is not in my own tomb
                    I shall lie . . .

. . . .

But if back there I could have known
                    this "now" of my life
I would have known
What it is
                 to be jealous . . .

Leningrad, 1944

CINQUE

Autant que toi sans doute, il te sera fidèle,
Et constant jusques à la mort.
Baudelaire

I

As at the edge of a cloud
I remember your words, your voice

You for whom because of my words
The nights were brighter than the days.

We were snatched from the earth
And walked the air with the stars.

And there was neither despair, nor shame, nor
remorse
Nor now, nor after, nor before.

But I am calling you,
Tell me, can you hear?

As if in life,
as if you were not dead,
The door you opened
will not swing shut.

November 26, 1945

II

Sounds decay in the ether,
Morning masquerades as shadow.
And the world is numb:
Only two voices —
                    yours and mine.
A wind
      from the invisible Ladoga Lakes
Brings the sound of bells
And our night's talk ends
In the weightless glitter
                    of crossed rainbows.

III

Always I detested it:
— Being pitied.
But with this single taste
                         of your pity
I walk with the sun in my body.
Because of this we are circled
                         by morning light
Because of this
               I create miracles.
Because of this!

December 20, 1945

IV

Surely you know that I do not celebrate
The bitter day of our meeting.
And what shall I leave you as a memento?
My shadow? What could you do with a shadow?
Or with the dedication of a burned-out drama
Even the ashes gone?
Or with a picture that suddenly steps from its
    frame,
That frightful picture of me in the New Year?
Or with the almost imperceptible sound
Of birch logs burning in the grate,
Or with—that thing no one quite fully told—
A love that was not mine?

January 6, 1946

V

We have not breathed the poppy.
We do not know our imperfection.
Under what heavenly signs have we been sent
Into the world, for our unhappiness?
What hellish broth
Served up by black January?
By what invisible shaft of fire
Brought screaming
                to the edge of day?

January 11, 1946

IN A DREAM

This black and endless
Separation:
I endure it too, everything —
Why are you crying? Come,
Give me your hand instead —
promise again
To come in dreams.

You and I
Are like grief and the mountain,
We will not meet
in this world.
But sometimes
will you send across the stars
A sign?

1946

SECRETS OF THE TRADE

I
Creativity

This is how it is: a restlessness
And a clock ticking louder and louder
in your ears
And far away the roll of receding thunder
And as in a dream
the complaints and groans
Of unfamiliar, captive voices;
The mysterious circle narrows
And among these whisperings and ringings
One all-conquering sound stands out
— Around it an irreparable quiet
And the rustle of grass growing in the wood —
And then walks boldly on
Strides over the earth carrying a knapsack.
Already there are distant words
And the small signal bells of light rhythms
And I begin to understand —
And with infinite simplicity, dictated lines
Lie down on the white pages of my notebook.

1936

II

Who wants battalions of impassioned odes
Or the beauty of elegiac enterprises?
My lines are all beside the point,
I don't see what others see.

And if you knew from what scraps
Poems are born — without shame
Like yellow dandelions by a wormy fence,
Like wild spinach or the common burr.

An angry cry, the fresh smell of tar,
A mysterious mould on a wall,
And the lines
        sing out
Audacious, tender,
        for your joy and mine.

1940

III
The Muse

How can I live with this handicap,
This madcap muse,
They say, "You are with her in Elysium . . . "
"What divine conversation . . . "

But she comes once
                like a wasting fever
And disappears for the rest of the year.

IV
The Poet

You call this work?
This carefree life:
To steal from music
And in fun make it your own.

To slip into your poem
Someone's happy scherzo,
And in fields flooded with light
Swear your lost heart groans.

And then to steal
From the forest,
From quiet pines
Circled by mist.

I steal and steal, right and left
And without shame,
A little from this impish life
And everything from silence and the night.

Summer, 1959
Komarovo

V
The Reader

He shouldn't be despondent
And especially, too closed up . . . no,
The poet should be open,
Clear to his contemporaries.

A ramp sticks up under his feet
And everything is death-like, empty, luminous.
The cold flicker of the lime-light
Brands his forehead.

But the reader is mysterious,
A buried treasure,
Even the least and most casual,
The one who never speaks out.

There, everything is,
          that nature had hidden
For her own convenience,
There at the appointed hour
Someone cries helplessly;

There what darkness of night,
What shadows, what coolness;
And unfamiliar eyes
Speak with me until morning.

They blame me for something,
They agree with me about something . . .
And then in the blessed noon heat of dialogue
A dumb confession comes.

Our time is swift,
Our given circle narrow,
But he is unchanging and eternal —
The unknown friend of the poet.

Summer, 1959
Komarovo

VI
The Last Poem

One interrupts like thunder
Rushes in the house
        on the breath of life
Laughs, trembles at my throat,
Pirouettes, applauds,
But another
        born in midnight silence
Creeps up from nowhere
Looks from an empty mirror
And mutters something angrily.

And others come like this:
in the middle of the day
As if scarcely seeing me,
They run along the white paper
Like a brook in a meadow.

And there is another one
who comes secretly
Neither sound nor color
Neither color nor sound.
He changes and twists
And will not give himself up
alive into my hand.

But this one! . . . this one drank blood
drop by drop
As a cruel young girl drinks love
And saying no word to me
became again — silence.

Cruel luck! He walks away
His shadow already touches unreachable barriers
And without him . . .
I die.

1959

VII
Epigram

Could Beatrice write like Dante?
Could Laura sing the heat of love?
I taught women to speak out . . .
God, how can I keep them quiet!

1960

VIII
About Poems

To Vladimir Narbut

They are the tag ends of white nights,
The black wick of bent candles,
The first morning bell
From a hundred white steeples . . .
The warm windowsill
Under the moon at Chernigoff,
Bees in the melilot.
They are pollen, obscurity, Canicula.

1940

IX
Secrets of the Trade

I dream of the carnation
        the pungent breath of the carnation
There, where Eurydice turns and turns
And the bull carries Europe over the waves
There, where our shadows fly
Over the Neva,
        over the Neva, over the Neva
There where the Neva splashes the steps —
This is your ticket to immortality.

1957

X

So much waits
To use my voice:
A certain wordless rattle
An underground rock in the dark
And something
That fights its way out
Through smoke.

My account's not settled
With fire
With wind, with water . . .
So that in light sleep
Suddenly, gates open up
And I go out
Toward the Morning Star.

1942

MISCELLANEOUS POEMS 1957–1964

You are with me again, friend autumn!
I. Annensky

Let others still find rest in the south
Renew themselves in the Garden of Eden.
This is the North
And I take Autumn
for my friend.

I live as if in someone else's house
A house that comes in dreams
And in which I have died perhaps
Where there is something strange
In the weariness of evening
Something the mirrors save for themselves.

I walk beside the short black pines,
The heather is like the wind
And a chip of new moon
Shines like a dull knife.

And I have carried here
the memory
Of our last meeting

the meeting we missed
And the pure weightless flame
Of triumph over fate.

1957

This too will become for the people
An age of Vespasian,
Only a wound —
And a cloud of suffering overhead.

December 18, 1964
Rome. Night

FROM "MIDNIGHT VERSES"

III
Beyond the Mirror

O quae beatam diva tenes Cyprum et
Memphin corentem Sithonia nive
Horatius

A pretty girl, rather young
But not of our century —
She is the third one,
We are never two people alone.

You draw up the armchair for her.
Generous, I divide the flowers with her . . .
What we do, we ourselves scarcely know,
But every moment we are more and more afraid.

Like people who've come from prison,
Each knows something terrible
About the other. We sit in some circle of hell
And it may be we're not even ourselves.

July 5, 1963
Komarovo

To M.Z.

I listen as to a distant voice
But there's nothing here, no one.
You will lay down your body
In this good black earth;

Neither granite nor weeping willow
Will shade your light ashes,
Only hurrying sea winds
                                    down from the gulf
Will weep for them . . .

Komarovo, 1958

A land not native
That stays in the mind
                    like a native land,
And in the sea, a water not salty
And caressingly cold.

The sand underneath
                    whiter than chalk,
And an inebriate air,
And the rosy body of the pine
Naked in the sunset.

And in this last light
                    on waves of ether
I can't tell if the day ends
Or the world, or if it is only,
In me again,
                    the mystery of mysteries.

1964

NOTES TO THE INTRODUCTION

1. There is available now a certain amount of material on Akhmatova, including translations into several Western European languages. The main source is Anna Akhmatova, *Works* (New York: Inter-language Literary Associates, 1967–68) 2 vols., second ed. (cited below as "ILA"). It has the original texts of all the poems and other material and has critical and biographical sketches and studies. Some of the best of this material is in English. Other available material includes Carlo Riccio, trans., *Poema senza Eroe e Altre Poesie* (Turin: Einaudi, 1966); Jeanne Rude, *Anna Akhmatova* (Paris: Seghers, 1968); Richard McKane, trans., *Selected Poems* (New York: Oxford, 1969); Paul Valet, trans., *Requiem* (Paris: Minuit, 1966); Raissa Naldi, ed., *Anna Achmatova: Poesie* (Milan: Nuova Accademia, 1962); Sophie Lafitte, trans., *Poésies* (Paris: Seghers, 1959); Renato Poggioli, *The Poets of Russia, 1890–1930* (Cambridge: Harvard, 1960); Howard William Chalsma, *Russian Acmeism: Its History, Doctrine, and Poetry* (Ann Arbor: University Microfilms, 1967).

   In the transcription of Russian names, we follow the *Encyclopaedia Britannica*, 1987 ed., with three exceptions. Akhmatova's beloved suburb of Leningrad is spelled below Tsarskoe Selo (not Tsarskoye . . .); her first husband's surname is spelled Gumilev (not Gumilyov); and the personal name of the poets Blok and Pushkin is spelled Alexander (not Aleksandr).

2. Riccio, p. 20.
3. Trans. Chalsma, pp. 48–50.
4. Chalsma, p. 51.
5. Dimitri Obolensky, ed., *The Penguin Book of Russian Verse* (Harmondsworth: Penguin, 1962), p. xlvi.
6. Trans. Chalsma, p. 105.
7. These stories can be found in Chalsma, pp. 52–53.
8. Poggioli, p. 225.
9. Cited from Wiktor Woroszylski, *The Life of Mayakovsky* (New York: The Orion Press, 1970), p. 273.
10. The translation of Gumilev's poem is by Lenore Mayhew.
11. According to Glebe Struve, *ILA*, p. 17 (note).
12. Poggioli, pp. 230–231.
13. The phrase is Riccio's, p. 12. Riccio has an excellent discussion of the change in Akhmatova's poetry that took place with *Requiem* and continued in *Poem Without a Hero.* See Riccio, pp. 9–17.
14. Riccio, p. 16.
15. Riccio, p. 17.
16. Riccio, p. 13.
17. This paragraph is adapted from LM, "Images from a Life," *Field* 39 (1988): 9–10.

18. For some discussion of the method, see William McNaughton, "Chinese Poetry in Untranslation," *Delos* I (1968), pp. 191–204; and Lenore Mayhew and William McNaughton, trans., *A Gold Orchid: the 'Tzu Yeh' Songs* (Tokyo and Rutland, Vermont: Charles E. Tuttle Co., 1972). Ernst Robert Curtius really establishes the theoretical basis for this approach to translation: see his *Europäische Literatur und Lateinisches Mittelalter* (Bern und München: Francke, 1963), pp. 10 and 21. The usefulness, to the translator, of such a work as Catherine A. Wolkonsky and Marianna A. Poltoratsky, *Handbook of Russian Roots* (New York: Columbia, 1961), can scarcely be exaggerated. Cf. William McNaughton, "Ezra Pound and Chinese Melopoeia," *Texas Quarterly*, X, iv (Winter, 1967), pp. 52–56, esp. p. 54. Georges Duhamel and Charles Vildrac, *Notes sur la Technique Poétique* (Paris, 1910), also have light to shed on the special problems faced by the translator of poetry. Finally, there are several pages in George Steiner's *After Babel* that bear on the method.

NOTES ON THE POEMS

Professor Silbajoris's contributions — see the Introduction — are marked "FS." In many cases not recognized below, Professor Silbajoris made contributions which we were able to work directly into the texts.

p. 40 The contrast here is between being a poet on the one hand, and breathing God's gift from the air on the other. The woman-poet matter is a simultaneous parody of the issue (FS).

p. 41 "To Alexander Blok": Blok, the finest of the Russian Symbolist poets, wrote the following poem on Akhmatova:

TO ANNA AKHMATOVA

They say to you, "Beauty is terrible,"
And lazy, around your shoulders,
You wind your Spanish shawl,
You tuck a red rose in your hair.

They say to you, "Beauty is simple,"
And awkward, with your many-colored shawl,
You cover a child
And the rose falls to the floor . . .

Distracted, you listen
                    to the words around you.
Sad, thoughtful
                    you say to yourself,

I am not so terrible
                    nor so simple as that,
Not terrible enough to kill simply
Or too simple to know
                    that life is terrible.

p. 45 The fifth line actually says "My insomnia that likes to sit around. . . ," but that, we fear, is about as translatable as Pound's "honest feathers" (of a Roman statesman's beard).

p. 46 With regard to the seventh line: it's like spreading out an obeisance, your prayerful respects, as if a carpet, before the altar. It immediately evokes the imagery of the flying carpet: the stuff of dreams of love transformed into a prayerful fairy tale, to contrast with the desert roads walked with the one you did not love. The epithet for "roads" also means the sort of distant places where the saints used to go to be near God, and founded monasteries, and gained fame for their humility. The word-associations in the context of Russian culture are absolutely wonderful (FS).

p. 77 Yezhovism: Yezhov was head of the Secret Police during the Stalin Period.

p. 80 They took you away at daybreak: she is writing about the arrest of Nikolay Punin in 1935.

Streltzys: the Royal Musketeers. Peter the Great had the officers executed in 1698, as he suspected them of treason. Peter himself attended and took part ein the executions.

p. 87 The blue cap: N.K.V.D. agents wear blue uniforms. — Yenisey: a river in Siberia.

The Fountain House: *i.e.*, the palace of Count Sheremetev on the Fontanka River. Akhmatova lived there from 1923–1941. "The Fountain House" was built between 1750–55 by the architects F.S. Argunov and S.I. Chevakinsky. Akhmatova also refers to it as "The Fountain Palace."

p. 89 The epigraph is in Slavonic.

p. 90 When the ashes of mourning are scattered upon the black curls of youth, the instant result is the silver of sorrowful old age — it is like a chemical metamorphosis, of both youth and time into the precious metal of a single moment at the terrible door of eternity. And remember — this happened to people who stood in front of the locked doors and unseeing red walls behind which their loved ones turned to stone in terror (FS).

p. 92 Sacred willow-tree: lit., "the stump of the sacred [or 'cherished'] tree." Does Akhmatova mean the tree about which she wrote the poem (p. 95) and after which she titled one of her books?

p. 99 The twenty-fourth play of Shakespeare: according to the local Shakespeare specialist, it is probably *Troilus and Cressida, i.e.* about the siege of Troy.

p. 100 To the Memory . . . : This is supposed to be an imitation by Akhmatova of popular ("people's") poetry.

p. 103 *Poem Without a Hero*: there are in circulation a number of versions of *Poem Without a Hero.* Every literatus of note in Moscow is supposed to have his own copy, differing in several respects from everyone else's. We have made a comparison of various versions. Where long sections have been absent from one text or another, we have included them if they seemed to us to add to the total effect of the poem. In case of textual variants of smaller units — of words or phrases — we have chosen between versions on the basis of intelligibility and literary effect. The ILA version seems to be the most complete. Riccio, however, makes the following claim for his text (his edition is bi-lingual, with the Russian text facing his Italian translation): "The text of *Poem Without a Hero* . . . represents a later and more complete phase [of the poem] than versions found in the various Soviet publications (only partial and fragmentary) and in the publication . . . in the magazine *Vozdúsnye puti* in New York in 1960 and 1961. In particular, the first part [is based] directly on a typescript given us by the poet herself. . . ; for the second part . . . and the third part, the poet herself gave us strophes, lines, variants, and stage directions (*sic*) to work into the text, and we have been able to consult the poet's manuscripts. So that our version is based on a text which can be considered virtually definitive. Our entire [Italian] translation of *Poem Without a Hero* was read and approved by Anna Akhmatova. Hence *Poem Without a Hero* is published by us, here, in Russian for the first time in its final form" (p. 21).

The ILA has the dates "1940–1962"; the legend "Leningrad-Tashkent-Moscow"; and the epigraph "*Di rider finirai / Pria dell'aurora.* / Don Giovanni" on its title page.

p. 107 This is a passage in Akhmatova's mock-simple style. Evergreen branches are spread on the path to the home of the deceased, around the coffin, etc. — the particular green smell of the dead that is so familiar to all East European children in their nightmarish memories. It is that smell, rising, that is being compared with the accumulation of sea foam as the waves of — what? eternity? oblivion? close in. In the context of the Russian Acmeists, this sea foam calls back to Mandelstam's wonderful poem "Insomnia and Homer. Sails drawn taut. . . ," where we have the line, "And on the heads of kings the foam divine," recalling all the way back to the mythological origins of that foam (FS).

The Fountain House: see the note above, p. 185.

p. 112 Riccio puts here, as the first epigraph, the "*Di rider finirai / Pria dell'aurora*" tag from *Don Giovanni*, and he does not give the *Don Juan* tag. The ILA text gives it (in English).

p. 113 And the wine burns like poison: "Why are my fingers soaked in blood / And why does the wine burn like poison?" (*New Year's Ballad*, 1923) (footnote to the Russian text).

p. 114 Dappertutto: Doctor Dappertutto, pseudonym of Vsevolod Meyerhold, mentioned in Hoffman's *Die Abenteur der Sylvester-Nacht*; Jokannon, *i.e.* John the Baptist (*sic*: acc. Riccio, p. 173); Glahn: Lieutenant Glahn, the hero of Knut Hamsun's *Pan*, kills himself for love.

p. 115 Not to me, but to. . . ?: the Russian here is *Ne ko mne, tak k komu zhe*?," and it is footnoted: "The three *k*'s express the author's confusion"; that is, Akhmatova has written a sort of stammer into her line.

p. 117 The oak of Mamre: the tree under which Abraham entertained God and three angels (Riccio says "and two angels"): *Genesis* 18.

p. 121 "The Dog," *i.e.* the cafe "The Wandering Dog." See the Introduction, p. 11.

p. 122 Chechetka: a rhythmic, toe-and-heel dance.

Ivanushka: "Johnny" — a character in Russian fables.

p. 124 Colleges of Peter: present site of the University of Leningrad, the building of the Twelve Colleges (the dicasteries of the epoch), built between 1722–42 by the architect Domenico Trezzini, is traversed by an extremely long corridor (Riccio note: p. 173).

The black and yellow banner flying: the "Imperial Standard" which was flown over the Summer Palace when the Czar was at court.

p. 127 Kellomiage: that is, the present Komarovo, where the poet used to spend her summers. She is buried there. Komarovo is on the northern shore of the Gulf of Finland, between Repino and Zelenogorsk.

The Malta Chapel: the Chapel of the Order of Malta, the work of Giacomo Quarenghi.

p. 128 *Skobar*: a pejorative name for an inhabitant of Pskov.

p. 130 Avdotya: popular name for Eudoxia. Eudoxia Lopukchina was the first wife of Peter the Great. She was opposed to his reforms and to the new capital. He repudiated her and sent her to a convent.

p. 131 The Cameron Gallery: built by the Scots architect Charles Cameron in the park at Tsarskoe Selo in 1783–86. The Nine: *i.e.*, the Muses (footnote to the Russian text).

p. 132 The ninth line is important because it points (somewhat distantly) to the clatter of the bronze hooves of the Bronze Horseman (Peter I — monument on the Neva, "Petro Primo Catherina Secunda"), as the statue chased poor Evgenij of *The Bronze Horseman* down the city streets (FS).

p. 134 The Masure, the Carpathian peaks: both of these were sites of great battles in the First World War; in both of them the loss of Russian lives was great. The Masure is a group of lakes in north-east Poland.

p. 137 These mileposts have stripes that make them look rather like a barber's pole. Akhmatova may have picked the milepost up from Pushkin, in which case Pushkin/milespost and Lermontov/ devil would make a very understandable pair (FS).

p. 138 Soft embalmer (in English in the original text): from Keats's "Ode to a Nightingale."

p. 140 And so the decades file by: The missing strophe and lines imitate Pushkin. Cf. "About *Eugene Onegin*": "Anyway, I admit with humility that two strophes were left out of *Don Juan*," wrote Pushkin (note in the Russian text). In Riccio's edition, the strophe beginning "And especially if I dream" does not appear at all.

p. 141 Luga: a city on the Luga River about 75 miles south of Leningrad. Riccio says, "Here, 'Luga' stands for any city far from Venice (the city of the Satin Domino) and of little importance to it" (p. 174).

p. 143 The seductive centenarian: the poet herself says that the "seductive centenarian" is a personification of the poem (note that in Russian, the word "poem" is of the feminine gender) (Riccio note, p. 174). See also the "Introduction," p. 23.

Bryullovian shoulders: the epithet is derived from the name of the Russian painter Karl Pavlovich Bryullov (1799–1852).

Star Chamber: that is, the English judicial tribunal (1488–1641).

The stanza beginning "— In the dark, under the pines of Manfred" is not in Riccio's edition.

p. 144 Clara Gazul: pseudonym of Prosper Mérimée (*The Plays of Clara Gazul*, 1825, was his first work).

p. 146 A certain star: Mars in the summer, 1941 (note in the Russian text).

p. 147 The cuckoo has stopped singing: the next seventeen lines are not in Riccio's text.

p. 148 Volkovo Field: a Leningrad cemetery.

"Sewed up": the monuments of Leningrad were protected during the war by special coverings.

p. 149 As she flew over Brocken at night: The old ending of the poem was: "But behind me, glowing with mystery,/ Calling herself 'The Seventh,'/ Rushing to the unprecedented feast . . . / Pretending to be a music notebook,/ The famous 'Leningrader'/ Returned to her native air" (footnote in the Russian text). "The Seventh," *i.e.*, the Seventh Symphony of Shostakovitch ("The Leningrad Symphony"). The composer, on October 1, 1941, took out in an airplane from the besieged city the first part of this symphony (Riccio, p. 174). In the three-page "autobiography" which she wrote ca. 1946, Akhmatova says that she flew out of Leningrad on 28 September 1941, which fits with "But behind me, . . . the famous 'Leningrader.' " See *Pamyati Anni Akhmatovoy* (Memories of Anna Akhmatova) (Paris: YMCA Press, 1974), p. 35. Other writers say that Akhmatova and Shostakovich were on the same plane.

p. 157 "Leningrad Elegy": a shorter version of this was published first with the title "From 'The Leningrad Elegy.' " The present version is printed in the group of "Northern Elegies" in the ILA *Works*, vol. I (pp. 308 ff.) where it bears only the title "The Third." It is, presumably, complete in this form. In the "autobiography" mentioned above, Akhmatova says, "In 1945 I wrote two cycles of verse, 'Cinque' and 'Leningrad Elegies,' and finished *Poem Without a Hero*."

p. 159 Cinque: the title is given this way, in the Roman alphabet, in the original text.

p. 160 The crossed rainbows, as I recall some of those

winter landscapes in Russia, would be glittering tiny icicles floating in the air in the sun, turning the whole sky and air into a fairy tale (FS).

p. 164 In Elysium: *lit.* "in the meadow."

ABOUT THE TRANSLATORS

Lenore Mayhew and William McNaughton have collaborated before, most notably on *A Gold Orchid: The Love Poems of Tzu Yeh* (1972). He is the author of many books on Oriental literature (*The Confucian Vision, The Taoist Vision, Light from the East, Chinese Literature: An Anthology*), and her most recent book is *Monkey's Raincoat (Sarumino): Linked Poetry of the Basho School with Haiku Selections* (Tuttle, 1985).